Under a full moon in the beautiful mountains of a little island a baby moose was born.

His fur was not at all like any of the other moose, it was a gorgeous shade of blue.

His parents, overjoyed to be blessed with such a special baby, named him Azure.

As Azure grew up he was well known throughout the forest.

Not just because he was blue but for his helpfulness and kindness,

He spent many hours searching for the squirrels lost acorns.

and helping his friend beaver build his dam.

One cool fall day Azure found a family of birds. Cold and hungry they were struggling to find a safe place after their nest was blown from a tree.

The little birds were so thankful to Azure, they told all the other little creatures of the forest that he was their protector, the protector of the little animals.

He often whistles a tune while he wanders along.

As each new summer and winter came and went Azure grew bigger and bigger.

Amazed by the way the ice on the pond made his reflection shimmer.

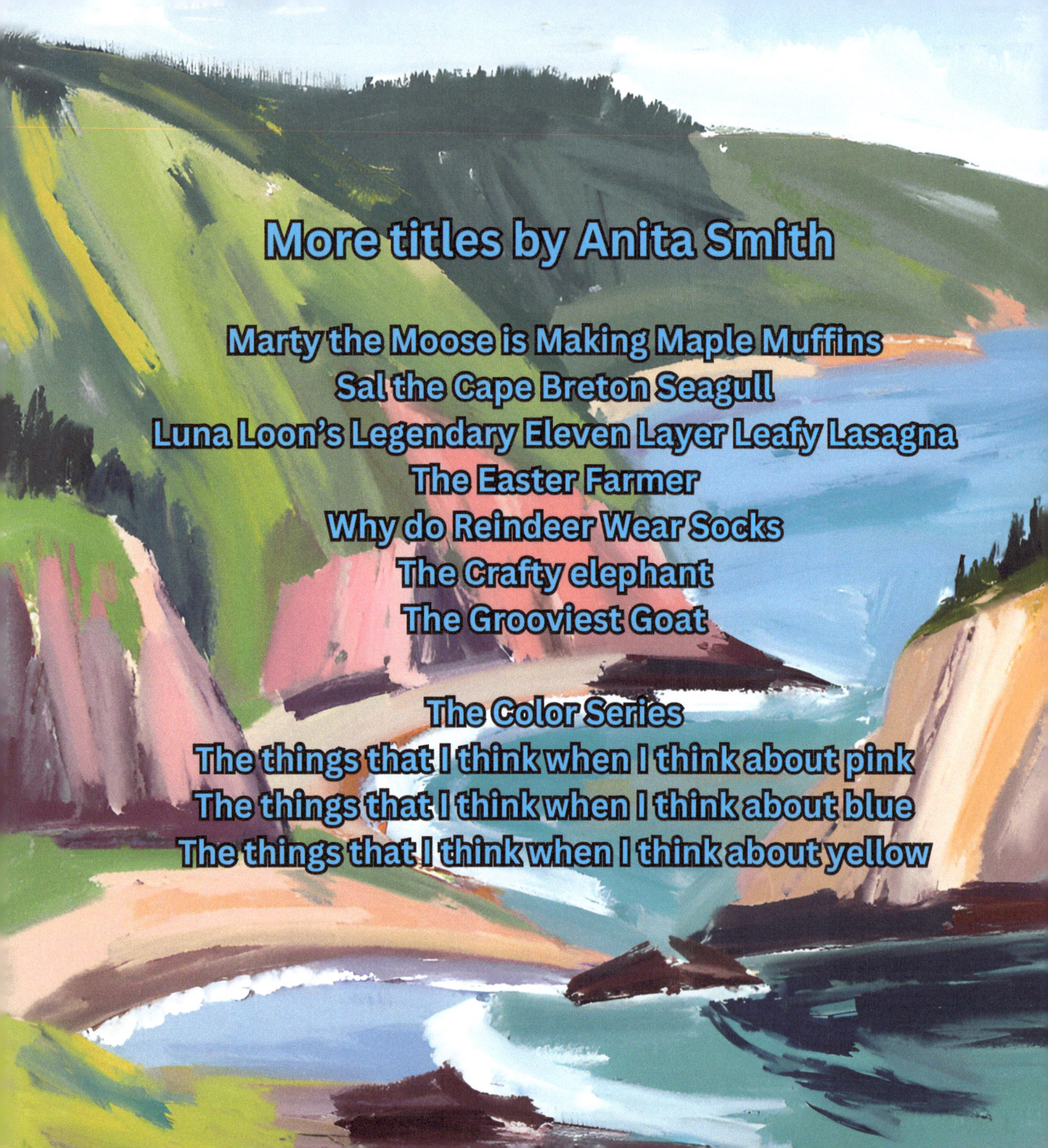

More titles by Anita Smith

Marty the Moose is Making Maple Muffins
Sal the Cape Breton Seagull
Luna Loon's Legendary Eleven Layer Leafy Lasagna
The Easter Farmer
Why do Reindeer Wear Socks
The Crafty elephant
The Grooviest Goat

The Color Series
The things that I think when I think about pink
The things that I think when I think about blue
The things that I think when I think about yellow

www.ingramcontent.com/pod-product-compliance
Lightning Source LLC
Chambersburg PA
CBHW041526070526
44585CB00002B/96